Social Psychology for Beginners

HOW OUR THOUGHTS AND FEELINGS INFLUENCE OUR BEHAVIOR IN SOCIAL INTERACTIONS

Lennart Pröss

Table of Contents

CHAPTER 1

Introduction to social psychology

Psychology in general concerns itself with the experience and behavior of humans. Social psychology concerns itself with the experiences and behaviors of humans in social situations. This short introduction into social psychology is meant to provide you with a rough overview of the topics that social psychology deals with concretely. The aim is to bring the most important areas of research and application closer to you. For this you will be introduced to the most diverse notions of common theories from all kinds of areas. Essential elements of chosen social psychological models will be presented to you. With the help of guiding questions, examples and small thought experiments, you will be invited to think about social psychological phenomena on your own.

The aim of this introduction is not to deal with individual theories to the last detail and to analyze them in their whole complexity. This is why especially chapters 2 and 3 of this introduction fall rather short. These two chapters are of a more theoretical and abstract nature but still an important foundation for the understanding of social psychologic research. This introduction, of course, does not replace a social psychological module at a university. It is more so intended to awake an interest in social psychology within you.

When it comes to content, all social psychological topics can be divided into four big processes. First of all, there are intrapersonal processes (chapter 3). Intrapersonal processes are processes that take place within one person. These processes include things like impression formation, social cognition or the rationale behind decisions. The second area of social psychology includes interpersonal processes (chapter 4). These are processes that take place between single persons. These include thematic areas like friendship, love and attraction. The third big area concerns itself with intragroup processes (chapter 5). Intragroup processes are processes that take place within a group of people.

Typical intragroup issues deal with group performance, the work ethic and decision-making within a group, as well as with authorities and majorities. The fourth and final big area of social psychology deals with intergroup processes (chapter 6). These are processes that take place between different groups. Relevant topics from this area are prejudices, conflicts and solidarity between group structures. You might have already noticed that social psychology is concerned with extremely relevant topics from the daily social life of every human being.

Due to this high variety of topics the range of professions of social psychologists is quite wide. Social psychologists work in the most diverse areas. Of course, they are active in the research of foundations and application. Social psychologists describe, research and analyze the most different areas of social life. They are teachers or more so tutors in the education of adults. You can find them in management consultation as well as in the research of market behavior and opinions. Even the advertising sector makes use of the expertise of social psychologists every now and then. Institutions of social welfare, such as juvenile welfare offices, social welfare offices or other social institutions, are dependent on the support of social psychologists as well. Last but not least, social psychology and its findings supports politics with advice and action. Groups representing interests, authorities and associations often make use of the expertise of social psychologists. You can see that the professional opportunities within social psychology are thus quite versatile.

In the field of social and behavioral sciences, social psychology can be seen as a linking factor. It connects processes on the so-called macro level with processes on the micro level. Macro processes are political, economic or socio-structural processes. They usually fall within the remit of political sciences, economics or sociology. Micro processes describe the subjective experience of the individual. These processes are usually dealt with by cognitive psychology, personality psychology or neuroscience. Social psychology eventually investigates how macroprocesses affect microprocesses and vice versa.

Before you can jump into the content topics of social psychology, chapter 2 will present the most important research methods, basic concepts of scientific theory and the quality criteria of social science research. Knowledge of these theoretic foundations is important for understanding the results of research. This chapter again will be kept quite short and, if you are interested, a more in-depth self-study is recommended.

Throughout the entire text you will find words in bold. If you enter those into an internet search engine or an (online) encyclopaedia, you will most certainly find in-depth literature on the respective subject area. In addition, important social psychological authorities are italicized. With a bit of luck, you will, at least partially, find their original works online as well.

One last note: For reasons of better readability this text will not explicitly reference both sexes. Thus, unless explicitly mentioned otherwise, both sexes are always meant. And now have fun with your introduction to social psychology.

CHAPTER 2

Research methods

Social psychologists basically deal with the same things that you deal with most of your life. As a rule, you try to recognize, predict and explain regularities in people's behavior. How should you best behave in situation X or why you prefer to help some people more than others are typical questions of social psychology that you encounter each and every day. However, unlike social psychologists, you do this in a non-scientific way. This means that insights, predictions, and explanations that a social psychologist makes must stand up to certain scientific criteria that do not matter to you in everyday life. In order to gain a better understanding of how a social psychologist conducts research, the following section will therefore first present the most important basic scientific theoretical concepts, quality criteria and research methods from the world of social psychology.

2.1 Scientific theoretical basic concepts

Every scientific theory is made up of **concepts and hypotheses.** Especially in the field of social psychology the exact **definition** of these terms is of enormous importance. This is due to social psychology often working with hypothetical constructs. Behind a **hypothetical construct** lies an abstract theoretical concept that cannot be directly observed or physically measured but can only be observed or derived with the help of **indicators.** It is, for example, not possible to directly measure the extent of prejudice in one person against a particular group of people. It is necessary to find indicators that make this hypothetical construct visible. In the case of prejudice, this could be derogatory remarks or gestures towards a particular social group. This process is called **operationalization.** If the hypothetical construct is adequately represented, one speaks of **construct validity**.

Hypotheses, on the other hand, specify the exact relationship between the individual hypothetical constructs. The relationship in socio psychological theories often takes the shape of an **if-then relationship**. If you identify yourself very strongly with a particular group, then your willingness to help other members of that group increases–this would, for instance, be a typical hypothesis from social psychological research. A more concrete example: You assume that a football fan of Arsenal would be more helpful towards another Arsenal fan than towards a fan of Manchester United. The hypothesis in line with this is: if two people perceive themselves as football fans of the same club, then their willingness to help each other is greater.

2.2 Quality criteria for the assessment of socio-psychological research areas

How good a theory ultimately is depends on a number of quality criteria. Within the scientific community very specific quality criteria, which are used to assess and analyse scientific theories, have become established overtime.

- **Internal consistency** – you should not be able to derive both a statement and its opposite from one theory

- **External consistency** – a theory should not contradict other, already proven theories without explaining exactly where and why those already proven theories are to be contradicted

- A good theory should make as **precise** explanations and predictions as possible

- A theory that can be **applied** to several situations is better

This short enumeration of quality criteria is by far incomplete but can give you a first impression of the high standards that a scientific (social psychological) theory must comply with. Many interesting theories are repeatedly subjected to severe criticism because they violate individual quality criteria.

2.3 Research methods of social psychology

After presenting how social psychological theories are developed and how their quality is assessed, the following will describe the methods which raise data and test hypotheses. The choice of the concrete research method in essence depends on the posing of two questions:

Should the data collection take place in the laboratory or in the field?

When data is **collected in the field,** it is collected in its natural environment. If one wanted to investigate the behavior of football fans, it would be a good idea to observe the fans directly in the football stadium. A big advantage of this data collection method is that the fans behave naturally in their "natural" environment. A major disadvantage, however, is that all external conditions cannot be controlled by the social psychologist.

The exact opposite is true for the **laboratory survey.** The external conditions are almost entirely under the control of the social psychologist, which is a great advantage for testing theories or hypotheses. A disadvantage of course is the "artificiality" of the situation. For example, it cannot be assumed that a football fan will behave in the same way in the laboratory as in the stadium.

In practice, these advantages and disadvantages often lead to a combination of field and laboratory research. Theories observed in the field are systematically tested in the laboratory. In the alternative, theories with their origins in the laboratory are tested for their probation in the field. You should understand both data collection methods in social psychology not as competing but as complementary methods.

Should data collection be used to describe, predict or explain a particular social phenomenon?

If the aim is mainly to **describe** a social phenomenon, usually means of **observation** and recording are used. If we stick to the example of the football fan, for example, fan culture with all its norms, customs and social structures can best be carried out by observing and recording fans in the stadium.

If, on the other hand, the goal is to **predict** a social phenomenon, the **correlation method** is usually the most common choice in social psychology. One speaks of a correlation study if two or more variables are systematically measured and an attempt is made to establish a relationship between them. An example of the correlation method could be, on the one hand, the measurement of a child's aggressiveness (collected through questionnaires to parents, teachers etc.) and, on the other hand, the simultaneous measurement of the average daily consumption of media violence, be it through watching television or playing computer games. Using special statistical methods that examine the correlation, it can then be analyzed whether there is a correlation between the child's aggressiveness and the daily consumption of violence in the media. However, caution is required when interpreting correlation studies. Correlation does not mean causality. This means that just because two things are observed at the same time, one does not necessarily cause the other. The causal relationship could also be reversed (the child is not aggressive because it consumes so much media violence, but the child consumes so much media violence because it is aggressive) or a third variable (e.g. parenting) could be responsible for the behavior.

If, however, one wants an **explanation** for a social phenomenon, the **experiment** is the preferred means of socio-psychological research. By systematically testing one variable against another, certain behavior can best be explained. For example, the aggressiveness of a child could be measured immediately before and immediately after the consumption of media violence and thus a causal relationship could be more easily identified than would be the case with a correlation study. Therefore, experiments, especially laboratory experiments, play a very important role in social psychology. The most common criticism of laboratory experiments its that they place the subjects in an artificial situation that does not reflect reality. As a result, the experiments lack realism. However, for the validity of the socio-psychological laboratory experiment, it is more decisive that the experiment possesses **psychological realism**. This means that the psychologically processed tests correspond to or strongly resemble those that occur in a real, natural situation.

2.4 Brief summary

Socio-psychological research deals partly with everyday social situations and partly very special social situations. It tries to describe, predict and explain the experience and behavior of people in those situations. Social psychologists use various research methods for this purpose. In order to obtain valid results from their observations, studies and experiments, they must adhere to the strict standards of the scientific community.

Now that you have gained an initial insight into the methods that social psychologists use in research, we move on to the content level. As already mentioned, all topics dealt with in social psychology can essentially be assigned to one of the following four areas: intrapersonal, interpersonal, intragroup and intergroup processes. What exactly lies behind these processes will be explained in more detail below. A selection of important theories and models will be presented to you and concrete examples will help you to understand the individual points.

CHAPTER 3

Intrapersonal processes

Intrapersonal processes are generally quite simply processing that take place within a person. This includes processes like impression building of other people (Why do you find this person attractive and not this one?), attribution (Why does this person behave this way in this situation and not differently? Is it due to the character or the circumstances?) and the rationality of decisions (Why do people often not act rationally in social situations?). The following chapter firstly deals with social cognition.

3.1 Social cognition

Social cognition refers to the process of acquiring, organizing and applying knowledge about oneself and the social world. These so-called **knowledge representations** are divided into different types in social psychology.

- A **scheme** serves as a tool to assign meaning to information that you take up in social situations. Schemes allow you to quickly find your way in a wide variety of situations and to behave appropriately without having to make great mental efforts. If, for example, your boss or teacher is talking to you, the scheme of listening better and not staring into the distance disinterestedly should be activated.

- A **script** is similar to a scheme but only refers to the chronological order of things. For example, when you visit a restaurant, you automatically know the chronological order of a typical restaurant visit through a script.

- A **category** is used to classify objects, people or events with similar functions or meanings. For example, a social category would be a classification by gender (man/woman) or by age group (child/adolescent/adult/senior).

- **Stereotypes** describe the general characteristics typical to the members of a social group or category.

- A **prototype** describes an ideal typical member of a social group. The ideal typical rocker combines all the general characteristics typical for the social group of "rockers". He, for instance, rides a motorcycle, wears a leather cowl, has long hair, etc.

These are largely all automatic processes that influence the experience and behavior of each individual in social situations. The constant comparison of the social situation with familiar schemes, scripts, categories, stereotypes and prototypes reduces your cognitive stress. But what other aspects affect your social thinking and information processing?

3.2 Underlying needs

The above-mentioned information processing has the function to serve basic needs.

- **The need to be accurate:** Many socio-psychological theories assume that people have an urgent need to develop a largely accurate picture of themselves and their social environment. The idea behind this is quite simple: if you have an accurate picture of your social environment and yourself, you can also make better decisions about your social behavior. In reality, however, you do not always find accurate information. Sometimes accurate information is not even desirable; for instance, if it conflicts with other needs.

- **The need for consistency:** People tend to look for information that matches their way of thinking, attitudes and opinions. But why do they do that? They try to avoid so-called **cognitive dissonance**. Cognitive dissonance actually means nothing more than having several mutually exclusive thoughts at the same time. This contradiction leads to an unpleasant feeling of inner tension. It can thus be that one simply wipes contradictions aside in order not to endanger one's inner consistency. For example, imagine you are a great supporter of a politician and you also vote for him regularly. In the meantime, however, information that in fact makes this politician unacceptable keeps surfacing. A lot of the time you will not actually change your mind about the politician but instead try to find justifications as to why this unacceptable behavior is not so bad after all. You do this (amongst other things) to avoid endangering your need for consistency and cognitive dissonance.

- **The need for positive self-assessment:** A number of socio-psychological studies have shown that people strive to protect or enhance their self-esteem. This means they also look for information that increases their self-esteem and avoid information that threatens it. This phenomenon can also be applied to the membership of a social group. If you belong to a political party, you will not go out of your way looking for information that could put your party in a bad light. On the contrary, you avoid such information and seek positive news about your party to protect your self-esteem. This already shows that this may contradict the need to be accurate.

These three needs of social information processing control not only the selection of information but also the way in which this information is processed.

3.3 Rationale behind decisions

Now that you have found out quite a few things about how people work through information in social situations, the question posed is whether people do this rationally. *Daniel Kahneman and Amos Tversky* concluded in extensive research that human decision-making processes are often, at least according to strictly mathematical or statistical points of view, not rational. They argue that humans divert from a completely rational behavior in three ways:

- **Probability Estimation**: The probability that a certain event will occur or not is often misjudged by humans. In doing so great probabilities are underestimated. Gambling providers, for instance, make intensive use of the phenomenon of false probability assessment.

- **Reference Point:** Humans tend to see the result of a decision in relation to a very specific point of departure; profits appear positive compared to this starting point and losses negative. A little example: imagine you find 10 EUR on the sidewalk. You are happy. Imagine now that you find 100 EUR on the sidewalk. Surely, your joy will be even greater. Now you can even find 110 on the sidewalk. Interestingly enough, the joy you feel will usually be greater when you find 10 EUR than the difference in your joy between finding 100 EUR and finding 110 EUR. This is despite the fact that both times the same amount of money (10 EUR) is found in addition.

In addition, small losses cause more negative feelings than small gains cause positive feelings. If you first lose 10 EUR and then later find 10 EUR again, you still have a slightly negative feeling due to the initial loss.

- **Framing the Decision**: A decisive factor when evaluating alternatives to decisions is the frame in which they are embedded. What exactly is meant by framing? For example, the assessment of a cancer treatment method is influenced by whether the respective risks are expressed in terms of survival or mortality rate. For example, a treatment may be assumed to have 75% survival rate, but the same treatment expressed with a 25% mortality rate may be rejected. The "survive" framework is far more positive than the "die" framework.

3.4 Impact of emotions and moods

Another factor with significant influence on our decision-making behavior in social situations is that of emotions and moods. In social psychology there is no uniform definition of the word **emotion**. In general, the word emotion can be understood as the feeling of a physical change that occurs upon perception of an exciting event. It is also because of this problem of definition that social psychology has increasingly concentrated on the effects of moods in social decision-making processes.

In contrast to emotions, one can define **moods** as follows according to *Bless*:

- Moods have a lower intensity than emotions.

- Moods are not directed at an object.

- The cause of a mood is not always the immediate focus of attention.

- Moods do not have certain reactions, such as a certain behavior, emotions or cognitions, as a consequence.

- Moods give information on the overall quality of the individual's own state.

In addition to one's own mind and the acquired knowledge, a person is also dependent on his feelings (emotions, moods) in order to analyze and interpret a social situation.

If a situation is perceived as normal, thus non-problematic, human beings can refer back to their previous knowledge (scheme, script, etc.) in order to act in an appropriate way. They are in a positive mood.

If, on the other hand, a social situation is identified as problematic, the picture changes. It is no longer possible for an individual to fall back on their existing knowledge. An individual in such a negative mood has to reassess the situation in order to adapt his further behavior and reactions to the social situation.

You might now think that people in bad moods are the better thinkers. That, in fact, is partly true. In investigations it could actually be stated that for positive and/or joyful humans the quality of arguments hardly plays a role. Even bad argumentation is trusted in a good mood. Meanwhile, it turned out that people in a sad, depressed mood do very well at paying attention to the quality of arguments. It has also been shown that people in good moods are much more likely to use stereotypes than people in bad moods.

This all does not mean that badly tuned people are better learners though. A good mood has a positive effect on creativity and problem-solving skills. The use of general knowledge structures (scheme, script, etc.) leads to a better flow of work and allows an individual to identify new contexts. The complete reflection-free integration into a smoothly running activity, which is under absolute control despite very high demands, is called **flow**. A good mood is also conducive to motivation. You have certainly already observed this in yourself. If you are in a bad mood, your motivation decreases faster during tasks and there is a danger that the task will be stopped completely. In summary, it can be said that a bad mood might lead to better cognitive expenditure, but creativity and motivation suffer drastically.

3.5 Attribution

It is also important for the interpretation of the social environment how you justify the behavior of your fellow human beings. *Fritz Heider*'s **attribution theory** provides an explanation for this. The theory says that you explain the behavior of people by ascribing the responsibility for action either to the situation or the disposition of the person. A distinction is therefore made between **internal attribution** (personality) and **external attribution** (situation). Imagine you have a new work colleague and he shows up late immediately on the first day. You can now attribute this behavior to the character of the new colleague and characterize him as unscrupulous, unreliable or even lazy. You could also, however, ascribe his behavior to external, situational factors. Maybe his car broke down, the bus or train did not come, etc. Both are absolutely possible logical explanations for his behavior.

When analyzing a person's behavior, however, people tend to overestimate the influence of personal disposition and underestimate the influence of the situation. This frequent misjudgment is called the **fundamental attribution error** in social psychology.

Besides the distinction of attribution in the location (internal and external) one can distinguish attribution on two further dimensions. On the one hand, there is stability. The cause for a behavior can be both stable and unstable. On the other hand, there would be the controllability. A behavior can be controllable and uncontrollable. These three dimensions of attribution can be combined at will.

To illustrate this *Bernard Weiner and colleagues* have compiled an interesting list of possible causes for success and failure in an examination:

- If the causes are internal, stable and controllable, **knowledge** is decisive for success or failure in an exam.

- If the causes are internal, stable and uncontrollable, **aptitude** is decisive for success or failure in an exam.

- If the causes are internal, unstable and uncontrollable, the **ability to concentrate** is decisive for success or failure in an exam.

- If the causes are internal, unstable and controllable, **effort** is decisive for success or failure in an exam.

- o If the causes are external, stable and controllable, **permanent resources** (e.g. help of a friend) are crucial for success or failure in an exam.

- o If the causes are external, stable and uncontrollable, the **task difficulty** is decisive for the success or failure in an exam.

- o If the causes are external, unstable and uncontrollable, **luck or chance** is decisive for success or failure in an exam.

- o If the causes are external, unstable and controllable, **temporary resources** (e.g. help from a stranger) are decisive for success or failure in an exam.

You see, for one and the same case there are a number of completely different types of attribution. Depending on the type of attribution, you can come to a different interpretation, opinion and evaluation of the social situation. While in other people, as mentioned above, one tends to attribute causes to character, one is more flexible in oneself. One likes to attribute one's own success in an examination to internal and stable factors. In case of failure, one prefers to blame external and uncontrollable factors. Among other things, this serves to protect self-esteem and self-confidence.

In the course of time, every human being develops a very specific style of attribution. A **style of attribution** is the relatively constant tendency of a person to use the same explanatory patterns in different situations. Seriously depressed people assign failures, for example, to constant internal, stable and controllable factors.

3.6 Impression formation and perception of persons

Everyone knows the saying, "You only get one chance at a first impression." This proverb is to clarify the importance of the **first impression** within the impression formation because a negative first impression seems difficult to disprove. Indeed, socio-psychological research confirms exactly this assumption. Although people generally form positive rather than negative impressions, a negative impression attracts a disproportionate amount of attention. It is also much more difficult to correct this negative impression with positive information. Conversely, however, this does not apply. Introduction of new negative information can much more quickly change the general impression given by the first impression in a negative direction. This might be connected to the fact that negative information is seen as the exception. Because of the higher rarity a higher attention is given to negative information and they are processed more intensively cognitively. The reasons for this could be evolutionary, since negative information could mean a possible danger for oneself. For example, if you find that your new colleague sitting next to you in the office has spent the last few years in prison, this will surely overshadow the fact that this new colleague has always made a nice impression.

The high value of first impressions is called the **primacy effect** in social psychology. This merely states that information presented first has an excessive influence on the overall impression. Thus, studies have shown that teachers rate students who solved the first of multiple tasks correctly but then made mistakes in the answering of further tasks better than those who solved the first tasks incorrectly and then performed the following tasks correctly.

The opposite case exists as well. The information last presented has an excessive influence on the overall impression. Social psychology calls this effect the **recency effect**. This recency effect, however, is usually the exception and occurs when a person is less motivated to process information.

Another effect that can occur during impression formation is the so-called **halo effect.** The halo effect means that knowledge of a certain characteristic of a person outshines all other characteristics. This could include character traits such as intelligence but also external traits like high attractiveness. A socio-psychological experiment showed, for instance, that essays by attractive authors were rated better on average than the same essays written by less attractive authors. Attractivity overshadowed the lower literary abilities.

Interesting socio-psychological phenomena that man unconsciously uses to maintain impressions are **self-fulfilling prophecies.** The self-fulfilling prophecy proceeds as follows: you have a certain expectation of the behavior of another person. Because of this expectation you treat that person in such a way that they are made to actually behave according to expectation. An example would be a teacher having the impression that a student is untalented. Because of this impression, the teacher treats that student in a very specific way. He, for instance, gives the student less time to answer a question because the teacher already assumes that the student cannot answer the question anyways. Due to this treatment, the student behaves nervously because he cannot answer the question correctly under the additional time pressure. Since the student cannot answer the question, the teacher's impression that the student is untalented is confirmed.

3.7 Brief summary

Intrapersonal processes are an important area of socio-psychological research. This area deals with a multitude of interesting topics from cognitive processes and their underlying needs, through the rationality of decisions and influence of emotions and moods on the individual, to attribution and impression formation. All these topics are the subject of current socio-psychological research. The insights and findings gained in this way play an important role in understanding how people understand their social environment and according to which patterns they develop social experience and behavior.

CHAPTER 4

Interpersonal processes

Interpersonal processes are processes between humans. The establishment, maintenance and development of social relationships have an extremely important significance for the subjective well-being of each individual. But what exactly is a social relationship? In social psychology one speaks of a social relationship when two people interact with each other and thereby influence each other in their experience and behavior. How close a social relationship is depends on several factors. Close relationships are characterized by the following points:

- A high degree of interdependence,

- The exertion of cognitive, affective and behavioral influence,

- This influence having a high intensity, and

- These traits lasting for a longer period.

But how does such a close social relationship develop?

4.1 From a fleeting relationship to a stable one

Mutual attraction is an important factor in developing a close social relationship from a simple social contact. **Interpersonal attraction** means to seek mutual contact, as it creates positive feelings within you. Attraction is thusly one step above sympathy. Even fleeting acquaintances can be sympathetic.

Which factors influence mutual interpersonal attraction?

- The frequency with which two people meet contributes significantly to their interpersonal attraction. The more often two people come into contact the more familiar they are with each other. The so-called **mere-exposure-effect** describes this phenomenon. As long as the first encounter is not negative, the repeated encounters have positive effects on the mutual attraction. However, if the first encounter is negative, more frequent meetings will intensify this negative feeling even further.

- A second factor contributing to closeness are the **character traits** of the other person. This includes their appearance, qualities, attitudes, preferences, etc. In the first encounter, the physical attractiveness is, of course, the most important factor. Within that, the face has a special position. The more average the face appears the more attractive it generally looks. In addition, people combine physical attractiveness with other positive qualities, such as intelligence or empathy.

- Another factor that plays a major role in interpersonal attractiveness is the **perception of similarities in relation to personally relevant attitudes**. There are several reasons for this. People with similar attitudes have greater opportunities to engage in similar activities, which can have a positive effect on the intensity of the relationship. People who are similar to you are likely to like you as well. Furthermore, perceived similarities in attitudes confirm one's own attitudes, which in turn makes you feel good.

- Your **own mood** is another factor that has positive effect on interpersonal attraction. If you are in a good mood, other people seem more likeable and attractive to you than if you are in a bad mood.

4.2 Types of relationship

Social psychology distinguishes between two different types of relationships: exchange relationship and community relationships.

In **exchange relationships,** the interaction between two individuals serves the exchange of material, social and/or psychological resources. People in an exchange relationship make the acceptance, maintenance or termination of the relationship dependent on how good the perceived cost benefit ratio is. This, of course, means that as long as the benefits of the relationship exceed the costs or no better alternatives are available, this interpersonal relationship will continue. The principle on which an exchange relationship is based is the **principle of equality**. When you do someone a favor, you expect a favor or something of similar value in return. Giving and taking should be balanced. Both partners pay close attention to this in such a relationship. Exchange relationships can usually be found between work colleagues, acquaintances, neighbors or strangers.

If the bond between both partners becomes stronger and stronger, especially on an emotional level, the relationship can develop into a **community relationship**. In a community relationship, both partners assume that each has the well-being of the other in mind. The focus is not so much on who gives and receives how much but on the needs of the other. A community relationship, therefore, functions based on the **principle of need**. This means, for instance, that you are willing to give something to your partner, even if you know they cannot reciprocate. Community relationships can be found in family relationships, close friendships or love relationships.

The transition from an exchange relationship to a community relationship is an important turning point in an interpersonal relationship. The transition is usually accompanied by self-revelations of sensitive information. One shares one's deepest thoughts and feelings with another, which strengthens the emotional bond, provided both partners reveal their thought processes. The self-revelation should not happen too early into a relationship; otherwise it can be more of a deterrent than emotionally binding.

4.3 The influence of interpersonal relationships on health

Numerous studies have found a positive correlation between social inclusion and both mental and physical health. Through the **experience sampling method**, social psychologists were able to demonstrate how a person's mood changes when visiting and leaving social encounters. The experience sampling method is a research method in which the test persons are encouraged to record their everyday moods in real time. They carry a notebook with them in which they record their feelings, moods or emotions on ready-made scales.

As you have, of course, already noticed, however, interpersonal relationships can also lead to negative feelings and moods. Conflict-laden relationships, the termination of a relationship or even the absence of social relationships can have extremely negative effects on well-being. Loneliness plays an extraordinary role. Lonely is the person who has fewer social contacts than they would like or who has relationships that are not of the desired quality. Loneliness, however, should not be confused with being alone. It is quite possible to be alone and not feel a bit lonely. Being alone can even be a beneficial pleasure. Overall, however, as mentioned above, good social relationships have a positive effect on mental health.

Physical health also benefits from good interpersonal relationships. Correlation studies have shown that socially involved people have better health. Emotional support (affection, appreciation etc.), instrumental support (material/financial) and support in decision-making and evaluation (feedback, information etc.) all have a positive effect on physical health. If this support is missing, this has demonstrably negative consequences for the immune system.

4.4 Maintaining relationships

A well-known model dealing with maintenance of relationships is the **investment model** of *Cyrl Rusbult*, which is based on the model of exchange relationships. A central point in this investment model is **commitment**. Commitment describes the intention to maintain a relationship, to feel emotionally bound to the relationship and to see oneself bound to the relationship partner in the future. According to Rusbult, the strength of commitment depends on three factors:

- **Satisfaction:** The more satisfied a person is with the relationship the greater their commitment. Satisfaction is made up of many different factors. The factors that can best predict satisfaction in a relationship have not yet been fully clarified in social psychology.

- **Investments**: In this context, investments are all factors that make ending the relationship relatively costly. These include resources such as money, time or emotions but also shared resources such as property (e.g. a shared house) or shared memories, friendships etc. The more resources that have flowed into and been produced in a relationship the higher the commitment.

- **Alternatives**: The presence of attractive alternatives, such as another partnership or even being alone, can lead to a decrease in commitment to the relationship.

A large number of studies have confirmed that these three factors influence the stability or instability of relationships.

4.5 Conflicts in relationships

Relationship conflicts often logically precede the resolution of relationships. This is often caused by communication problems, which in turn can further complicate the solution of the actual problem. Often, two very specific communication patterns are found in disturbed relationships.

- **Reciprocity of negative affectivity**: What does this mean? The principle is very simple. An act or thing is rewarded with the same. If your partner frowns critically, so do you. If the corners of their mouth go down, so do yours. Every negative sign of your partner is answered with a similar negative sign from you. This creates a dangerous negative spiral in conflict situations.

- **Communication need vs. Retreat interaction patterns**: This communication pattern is based on the different confit management patterns of the different sexes. In conflict situations, men tend to retreat and approach problems as rationally as possible. Women, on the other hand, act extensively based on their current emotions and are very expressive and communicative. These two conflict management strategies of man and woman are fundamentally different, with neither being better or worse than the other. The problem is simply that the two strategies do not go well together.

Another point that can intensify conflicts in relationships is the **attribution** mentioned above. If, in a happy relationship, your partner is completely irritated and comes home from work in a bad mood, the external factors, such as the situation, are attributed. Maybe your partner was stuck in traffic or had trouble with a work colleague. In a critical relationship, on the other hand, you attribute the irritability and bad mood to their character. Your partner is a bad-tempered grump. If you are understanding and supportive in the first situation you can improve your partner's mood. In the second situation you blame your partner for their bad mood, potentially making the situation even worse. A vicious circle of conflicts might occur.

4.6 Prosocial behavior

In social psychology behavior is referred to as prosocial if society considers it profitable or advantageous for other people/society. It is positive behavior through and through. Therefore, it is not surprising that social psychology and other scientific disciplines deal intensively with the question of when and why people help other people. Through research on prosocial behavior one hopes to gain knowledge about human nature and how to motivate people to more prosocial behavior. Prosocial behavior is always extremely context-dependent. Slapping someone in the face in isolation would certainly not classify as prosocial behavior. However, if this is done to help another person in dire need, physical violence for instance could be extremely prosocial.

How exactly is helping defined in social psychology? **Helping** is the term used to describe behavior that a person carries out with the intention of improving or protecting another person's situation or well-being. It is crucial that this behavior is intentional. *Pearce and Amato* have developed a classification system that allows help to be classified in three independent dimensions. These three dimensions are:

- **Degree of planning:** Is the help behavior relatively spontaneous and informal or is it planned in the long run and formal? A spontaneous, informal help behavior exists, for example, when you pick up an item that someone has dropped. A planned, formal behavior can often be found in voluntary work. For instance, if you train the youth soccer team in your district, the help behavior is planned.

- **Degree of difficulty:** Does the help serve a smaller problem or is it help with serious consequences? Giving a person change or holding the door open is certainly a small help. However, if you give first aid after a traffic accident in order to possibly save a human life, the enormous extent of this help is obvious.

- **Type of contact:** Is the contact for the helper direct or is the help being provided indirectly or mediated? Take, for example, a storm that devastates parts of your neighboring city. You can now, for example, help directly and abruptly by driving into the city and helping with the clean-up work. Or you could donate money or goods and thus help indirectly.

You can see that helping others can be understood as a wide variety of actions that differ massively in their quality. Up to now, help behavior has only been examined from the helper's point of view. The recipient may even regard well-intentioned help as an insult or feel dependent. You should therefore always keep an eye on the feelings of the recipient of the help in the case of prosocial behavior.

The concept of helping is to be distinguished from the concept of **altruism.** The primary goal of altruistic help is to protect and/or improve the well-being of another person. Helping is absolutely selfless. The personal benefit for the helper, e.g. social recognition, arises only casually and is not intended.

Altruistic help thusly stands in contrast to **egoistic help**, which primarily aims to improve or protect the welfare of the helper. The welfare of the help recipient only comes in second place.

Why do people help each other?

After the previous discussion of the types of pro-social behavior that exist, we now turn to the more specific motivations as to why people help each other in the first place. This has, amongst others, **evolutionary reasons**. Natural selection furthered prosocial behavior. Helping the immediate family promotes the indirect reproductive success of the individual. *Meyer* calls this phenomenon "**relative selection**", which is based on *Hamilton*'s concept of overall fitness. There is a great number of empirical evidence for the assumption that help behavior increases linearly the higher the degree of kinship between helper and recipient there is. Interestingly enough, this relationship occurs mainly in life-threatening situations.

People also help people unrelated to them. How does this happen? The **principle of reciprocity** often plays an important role in this regard. If you help a non-relative, there is a chance that they will return the help at a later point in time. For example, if you are good at maths in school, you can help a classmate prepare for the exam. In return, you hope to get help when it comes to preparing for your literature exam.

Furthermore, help behavior is often based on simple cost-benefit analysis. The human being follows the principle of benefit maximisation. When making a decision regarding helping a person or not, people consider various consequences:

- **Material consequences:** What costs occur for you (financially etc.) when helping somebody? What is the material/financial reward if you help this person?

- **Physical consequences**: What efforts, pains or even injuries do you have to put up with to help a person? Does helping benefit you physically in the long run (e.g. if volunteering to supervise a sports team)?

- **Social consequences:** Do you have to worry about negative social consequences if you help the other person? These consequences could be exclusion or ridicule. Or do you benefit from helping and are given recognition?

- **Psychological consequences:** Do you have to fear negative consequences if you help another person? This could include overcoming fears or disgust. Or does your help behavior benefit you on a psychological level, e.g. through increased self-esteem or the reduction of negative feeling?

But not only has helping certain costs and benefits, **not helping** can also carry its own benefits and costs. Therefore, humans also compare the costs of helping with the costs of not helping. *Jane Piliavin and colleagues* have identified possible behavioral reactions of potential helpers with regard to the expected costs of helping and not helping:

If both the costs of helping and those of not helping are low, the help behavior of people varies according to their personal norms. If the costs of helping are low and those of not helping are high at the same time, people usually help as directly as possible. If the costs of helping are high and those of not helping are low, most people ignore, deny or leave the situation without helping. And finally, if the costs for helping as well as for not helping are high, the person tries to help indirectly or to reinterpret the situation.

You can see that helping and non-helping is often a complex cost-benefit analysis. But help behavior is not always based on such calculations. Sometimes people simply help others out of **empathy**. Empathy includes feelings such as compassion, concern, sympathy, caring or warmth that arise from taking on the perspective of the person who may be in need of help. Such empathy-based help behavior is facilitated by a sense of attachment between the helper and the person in need of help.

Daniel Batson and colleagues performed an interesting experiment regarding the effects of empathy on help behavior: the so-called **Elaine-experiment**. In this experiment, the test subjects were given the impression that Elaine (an accomplice of the test leader) was supposed to solve learning tasks under stress. The stress was caused by supposed electric shocks in case of wrong answers given. Elaine suffered greatly from those electric shocks due to a childhood trauma. The test subjects now had the opportunity to take over the role of Elaine in order to relieve her of her suffering. The result was that people who had a higher resemblance to Elaine felt more empathy and were more willing to help her.

An interesting finding can also be observed in the different help behavior of the two sexes. Women help in the shape of care and commitment, while men usually are more inclined to help in emergency situations.

So how come time and time again people do not help others in emergency situations?

Latané and Darley have set up a model that shows which steps a witness to an emergency has to take in order to help. Those steps are:

- The witness must notice the emergency.

- The witness must interpret the emergency as such.

- They must take responsibility.

- They must choose the appropriate type of assistance.

- They must ultimately implement the decision.

The problem is that it is easy to fail at all of the five steps and not help at all as a result. Just noticing the emergency is not always possible. If a violent car accident happens under your nose, you will certainly notice it. If, however, a man with a heart condition slowly collapses on a park bench and you are using your mobile phone, you may not even notice an emergency is occurring.

Let us assume that you do notice the man collapsing for the sake of this essay. Now you have to be able to interpret this scene as an emergency. The next step would be for you to take responsibility and help. But why you out of all people? There are a dozen other people around you who could help just as well or maybe even better. In social psychology this phenomenon is called diffusion of responsibility. The responsibility to intervene in an emergency situation decreases with the presence of other people.

Let us say you do take responsibility. What is the right kind of help now? Do you address the person first? Do you address other passers-by? Do you call an ambulance directly? The right kind of help is not always obvious. But even if you have now successfully taken the first four hurdles, you still have to implement your theoretical plan. Being unsure of what the right kind of help is can have an extremely inhibiting effect and lead to the termination of the help.

4.7 Aggressive behavior

Social psychology defines aggressive behavior as follows: aggression is a deliberate behavior that aims to harm another person in any way, while this other person tries to avoid it. What is interesting about this definition is that the very intention of harming someone is enough to evaluate aggressive behavior as such. If you try to hit another person but fail, this will still constitute aggressive behavior.

Furthermore, aggressive behavior, as well as prosocial behavior, is strongly contextual. Aggressive behavior, for instance, can be seen as prosocial if you have to defend a third person in an emergency situation.

What forms of aggressive behavior can be distinguished in social psychology?

A distinction is made between:

- **Physical aggression** (e.g. hitting somebody) **and verbal aggression** (e.g. cursing at somebody)

- **Open aggression** (e.g. attacking somebody directly) and **hidden aggression** (e.g. gossiping behind someone's back)

- **Aggression between individuals** (e.g. a simple brawl) and **aggression between groups** (e.g. a mass brawl between opposing football fans)

- **Hostile aggression** (usually the result of negative emotion, such as anger or fury, with the sole aim being damaging another) and **instrumental aggression** (aggression serves as the means to an end)

What are the reasons for aggressive behavior?

Over time, social psychology has developed various explanatory models for aggressive behavior. The **frustration-aggression hypothesis** is a well-known explanatory hypothesis for aggressive behavior. Frustration occurs when a person is prevented from achieving their desired goal or when a certain event fails to provide the expected result and satisfaction. This frustration can then lead to aggressive behavior towards other people. The frustration tolerance is different for each individual. What makes one person angry can leave another completely cold. The frustration tolerance is also strongly dependent on the situation. It is also interesting that the exercise of aggression depends on feared sanction possibilities of the goal of aggression. You would certainly not physically attack a person who was physically far superior to you, as you would have to fear that you would lose out in a direct confrontation. In practice, this often leads to a so-called **aggression shift.** With the aggression shift a third person gets to feel aggression because the original source of frustration is not attackable.

The **cognitive-neoassociationist perspective** goes one step further than the frustration-aggression hypothesis. According to the cognitive neoassociationist perspective, an event that triggers a negative effect is responsible for aggressive behavior. This non-specific negative effect activates a series of cognitions, feelings and memories associated with either aggressive behavior or escape behavior. These thoughts, feelings and memories are then systematically processed and lead either to anger and irritation (aggression) or to fear.

Often, however, aggressive behaviors are also simply learned. Two specific learning principles are of great importance in social psychology for the acquisition of aggressive behavior: operant conditioning and model learning. In **operant conditioning**, aggressive behavior is learned through direct reinforcement. This means that the occurrence of aggressive behavior is reinforced by positive behavioral consequences. Suppose you intimidate your little sister so much that she always gives you her chocolate. The aggressive behavior (intimidation) leads to a positive behavioral consequence (preservation of chocolate), which increases the likelihood of a similar behavior occurring in the future.

Model learning is another process by which aggressive behavior is learned. Model learning means that through observation of the aggressive behavior of another person, who is rewarded for the same behavior in one way or another, the same behavioral pattern is learned. So, if you observe your father asserting his will by shouting at your mother wildly you run the risk of adopting this behavior because it is successful. In the future, you will try to enforce your will in a similarly aggressive way. Both theories for learning aggressive behaviors have been confirmed in numerous studies.

Are there gender-specific differences with regard to aggressive behavior?

There are differences in both frequency and manner. Men, as crime statistics show, are over-represented in violent crime. They tend to be more openly and physically violent. Women, on the other hand, tend more towards hidden aggression. Women are, for example, more likely to spread rumors aimed at harming another person. Overall, a meta-analysis by *Bettencourt and Miller* showed that men generally react more aggressively than women. However, if provocations come into play, women react as aggressively as men. The again, men feel provoked faster than women do.

Does media consumption glorify violence and have an effect on aggressive behavior?

Research provides quite a clear picture: the occurrence of aggressive behavior is increased by the consumption of violence in the media. This is true with regard to both short and long term. This connection, though, is moderated by the personality of the individual and the respective situation. People who are aggressive by nature are more strongly influenced in their own aggressiveness by the consumption of violence in the media. Consumption has a stronger effect on aggressive behavior for boys than for girls.

What is the best way to reduce interpersonal aggressive behavior?

Since frustration is often caused by an interaction, **apologies** are a simple and effective method to prevent aggression. The effectiveness of an apology depends on two factors. Firstly, the worse the frustration-triggering event is the stronger or more extensive the apology must be in order to have an effect. If you, for instance, damage someone else's expensive new car, a simple, "Oops, sorry," will not be enough. Secondly, the apology must be serious, genuine and presented in a credible manner.

The presumably most common social measure to reduce or prevent aggressive behavior is **punishment** or threats thereof. Social psychologists agree that punishment is only effective if the following conditions are met:

- The punishment must be sufficiently unpleasant.

- The punishment must follow aggressive behavior with a high probability.

- The punishment must have a comprehensible connection to the misconduct, for the punished person to see and understand.

- The punished person must recognize that they could have acted differently, which would not have resulted in punishment.

- The punishment must be properly proportioned, especially for children.

Anti-aggression training can prove helpful in preventing future aggressive behavior. Through role plays and various exercises, participants are intended to learn the following **anger management skills:**

- The recognition of the trigger of anger ("What made you angry in this situation?")

- The practice of a calming self-talk ("Keep calm, take it easy.")

- Learning alternative behaviors (e.g. relaxation techniques)

- The acquisition of skills to communicate dissatisfaction and anger correctly and to signal willingness to compromise ("The following has frustrated me in the situation. What can we do to prevent this from happening in the future?")

A prerequisite for the success of anger management training is the participant's insight that their aggressive behavior is the wrong approach and motivation to want to change this behavior in the future. Otherwise, such trainings are futile and have little chance of success.

CHAPTER 5

Intergroup processes

In social psychology, intergroup processes describe processes that take place within a group of people. Groups have always been important for individuals. People work together in groups to achieve goals that they could not achieve alone. Groups help the individual to orientate himself with regard to the appropriateness of his thoughts, feelings and attitudes. Groups provide a point of reference for norms and values. Furthermore, groups provide the individual with a part of his identity. In short, living and working together in groups is of great importance to the individual in daily social life. The following section gives a brief overview of what groups are, how they are formed and how to socialize in groups.

5.1 The social group

What exactly is a social group? A **social group** is a group of individuals who perceive themselves as members of the same social category and at the same time share an emotional attachment to their common self-definition. When using this group term, it does not matter how large the group ultimately is. Both small groups, such as a working group in which direct face-to-face communication is possible between all members, and large **social categories** (such as, for instance, British people, tax consultants, students, etc.) in which there is no direct interaction are considered social groups. **Entitativity** is the term used in social psychology when a group of people are even perceived as a coherent social unit by an outside observer. Groups with very close interactions such as families or teams thus exhibit a high entitativity. In this context, **group cohesion** refers to the inner cohesion of a group—the so-called "sense of togetherness". This cohesion is evident in the high intensity and emotional bond between the group members. **Social identification** describes the psychological relationship between the individual and his group. The higher the significance of the group membership for the individual, and the more emotions the individual invests in the group, the greater the social identification with the group.

What are the reasons for group formation?

There are different explanations for this depending on the perspective:

- **Evolutionary psychological approach**: Living together in groups has given people a greater chance of survival. As a result, humans have developed an innate need to belong to a group (keyword: natural selection). This approach is supported by the fact that people from different cultures and societies have always formed groups. Group formation has an adaptive value according to the evolutionary psychological approach.

- **Exchange and interdependence theoretical approach**: This approach emphasizes the interdependence of people. The formation of groups makes it easier for people to exchange resources and to tackle the achievement of goals together. Group formation thus serves to satisfy individual needs. The exchange and interdependence theoretical approach is thus an instrumental one.

- **Social identity approach:** People strive to obtain a positive self-image of themselves. A not inconsiderable part of this self-image comes from membership in a social group and the evaluation of this membership. The self-image results from the comparison of one's own group with other social groups. Accordingly, the comparison can turn out positively or negatively. The social identity approach is thus a cognitive approach.

- Of course, these three approaches should not be regarded as mutually exclusive but rather as complementary. They are merely intended to show different perspectives from which social psychology looks at group formation.

How exactly does a group function?

Compliance with norms is an important factor for the functioning of groups. Social standards can be described as follows: social standards are expectations shared by all group members. They determine how to best behave and how not to behave in certain social situations. They also specify what opinions, attitudes and feelings are socially appropriate or inappropriate. Those who behave according to the norms are socially rewarded; those who violate them are socially punished. Norms are not universal but socially determined and vary from group to group.

Here is an example from football: imagine you are a member of a fan club of your favorite club. In this fan club there are certain norms. You have to support your own team unconditionally, you are hostile towards other teams etc. In the stadium you have to abide by certain rules, customs and rituals. You are expected to behave in a certain way during certain events—cheering on your own team, whistling out the opposing team or singing along to certain fan chants. If you do not follow this behavior, you will at least be punished with critical glances; in the worst case you will be expelled from the fan club. If you follow the norms, you remain part of the group, which can help you achieve a positive self-image.

What functions do norms fulfil in social groups?

- **Group locomotion:** In group locomotion, the norms ensure that the group members have the same goals they want to achieve.

- **Group maintenance:** Norms help to stabilize the behavioral expectations between group members, which can lead to satisfactory interactions between group members.

- **Interpretation of social reality:** Norms provide a framework for evaluating events and behaviors.

- **Definition of the relationship in the social environment:** Norms define the identity of the group. This serves to define and distinguish other groups.

When social psychology analyzes the behavior of individuals, it also makes sense to distinguish two different types of norms. First, the **injunctive norm**. This states which behavior is approved by others and which is not. Second: the **descriptive norm**. It states which behavior is considered meaningful or appropriate. It is based on the motto: "If everybody can do it, so can I."

Furthermore, **social roles** have to be distinguished from social norms. Social roles define the expectations shared in a group, how a certain person has to behave in a certain role within the group. A social role can, for example, be a professional role (e.g. boss) or a family role (e.g. mother).

How does a typical group socialization process work?

The psychologists *Richard Moreland and John Levine* have developed a model in this regard that refers to groups that communicate directly with each other, exist over a longer period of time, and where individual members are interdependent. A typical example of such groups would be a sports team or project group. The model divides **group socialization** into five phases:

First phase – exploration: In the exploration phase, an existing group searches for members and individual humans search for a group. The aim of both searches is to find someone to satisfy their needs. In the case of a sports club, the individual is looking for an environment in which they can play sports, and the club is looking for reinforcement for one of its teams. If both parties think that the other can satisfy their needs, the individual enters the group. Often the entry has a formal character, which can be understood as a kind of rite or ceremony (e.g. the issuance of the membership card). With the entry into the group, the exploration phase ends.

Second phase – socialization: In the socialization phase both parties try to interact in such a way that the relationship is profitable for both sides. The group influences the new member in such a way that it contributes to achieving the group's goals (e.g. winning the next game). The new member is taught the usual norms and rules and assigned a social role in the group. The individual in turn tries to influence the group in such a way that his own needs are met by the group. If this interaction is satisfactory for both parties, the new member becomes a full member of the group.

Third phase – maintenance: In the maintenance phase, the focus is on the group membership. Both parties negotiate changes in the role of the individual (e.g. the individual wants a more responsible position in the team). This new role should continue to serve the goals of the group and the satisfaction of individual needs. The more profitable this negotiation process is for both sides the higher the commitment to the group will be.

Fourth phase – resocialization: If the member fails to meet the group's expectation, the group's commitment to the member may diminish. If, on the other hand, the group fails to meet the member's need, the member's interest in the group may also diminish. Both can lead to the member losing his role in the group. They are degraded to a marginal member. Subsequently, attempts to re-socialize the group or the individual are made. If the desired success is not achieved, the member may leave the group or be requested to leave it. Exclusion from a group that is important to the individual can have serious psychological consequences for the individual if the group membership places very high value on the self-image of the individual.

Fifth – memory: In the memory plans, both the former member and the group retrospectively evaluate their relationship. Both parties hold on to the relationship in some way if the relationship was seen as positive or profitable overall.

5.2 Social influence

When other people's opinions, attitudes and behaviors influence and change your own opinions, attitudes and behavior, social psychology speaks of social influence. The three most common forms of social influence are presented below: majority influence, obedience and minority influence.

Majority influence

Majority means nothing but the overarching general populous. The change of individual attitudes, behavior etc. by social influence of the majority is called conformity. Your own positions are adapted to those of the majority. Why does a numerical majority influence an individual's attitudes, values, behaviors, etc.? Social psychology has identified two different processes of influence:

The informational influence

In the information influence, the individual accepts the attitudes, values, etc. represented by the majority as the correct interpretation of reality. Especially if you are very unsure how to evaluate a (social) situation, you orientate yourself by the judgments or behavior of the majority.

Muzafer Sherif conducted an interesting experiment on informational influence. He had his subjects observe a fixed point of light in a dark room. Due to the so-called autokinetic effect, the subject feels as if the light spot is moving, although it remains fixed in one and the same place all the time. The test subjects were asked to indicate how far the light spot had moved in their opinion in a series of passes. If the test person went through the passages alone, the values oscillated around a personal estimated value. The estimated value visibly differed between the individual test subjects. If, however, the test subjects were questioned in the group, a group norm settled down after a few rounds and the personal assessment was abandoned. Even if the test subjects were then questioned again alone, they continued to orient themselves towards the group norm. They adopted the estimation of the group as an appropriate interpretation of reality.

The normative influence

With normative influence the effort of the individual is to avoid behavior deviating from the norm. This is done in order to meet the expectations of the group/majority or to avoid negative sanctions.

Salomon Asch impressively explained the normative influence in his conformity experiments. The test subjects were to compare three lines of different lengths with a reference line repeatedly and indicate which of the three lines had the same length as the reference line, a very simple task that 95% of the test persons could solve without any errors. In the experimental group, the individual test subjects were assigned to a group in which each person made their judgment one after the other. The test person was the last to give their verdict. The other persons were accomplices of the experimental management, who unanimously and publicly made false judgments. As a result, 37% of the test subjects' decisions were wrong. Only 24% of the test persons were not at all impressed by the judgments of the other persons and answered all tasks correctly.

In social psychology, the behavior that conforms to standards without accepting this standard in private is called **compliance.**

There are a number of different situational conditions that favor normative influence. The most important are:

- **Size of the majority**: The size of the majority is not as decisive. What is important is that the identifiable majority has a different opinion so that normative influence can be exerted on the individual.

- **Unanimity of the majority**: The majority unanimity plays an important role in normative influence. Asch was able to determine in further experimental arrangements that deviation of the majority could reduce that same influence.

- **Independence of sources**: Several independent sources of information are regarded as more convincing than a single group judgment and thus exert a higher normative pressure on the individual. For example: If three newscasters of one and the same channel present a dubious message to you, this has less normative influence on you than if three newscasters of three different channels present this message to you.

- **Interdependence**: The more dependent the individual group members are on each other the higher the normative influence they exert on each other.

Obedience

While majority influence is the influence of members of a group with the same status, obedience is the influence of an **authority**. Authorities are people with a higher status who are either given higher expertise in a field or have the ability to give out sanctions. Obedience, like majority influence, can thus be divided into normative and informational influence. In the case of informational influence, special competence is ascribed to the authority, which entitles it to demand obedience. In the case of normative influence, the authority has the possibility of sanctioning the individual if he or she does not obey.

Stanley Milgram conducted the most well-known experiments on obedience to authorities. In the **Milgram experiments**, the subjects were placed in the role of the teacher, who was supposed to apply electric shocks to their students if they answered a question incorrectly. They were led to believe that the effects of punishment on learning should be investigated. The student was an accomplice to the investigator and the electric shocks were not real. The subjects, though, were left in the belief and were given a quite painful 45-volt electric shock to give them a feeling for the alleged situation of the student. The electric shocks started at 15 volts and increased by another 15 volts up to 450 volts with each wrong answer from the student. From 75 volts the student screamed in pain; from 150 volts he asked the subject to stop the experiment. However, the experimenter instructed the subject to continue. More than 60% of the test subjects were thus prepared to apply even the highest dosage of 450 volts. The subjects obeyed the investigator. Milgram's experiments yielded a lot of important findings regarding obedience to authorities. At the same time, the experiments also triggered ethical controversies about what psychological research is allowed to do and what it is not. After the experiment, the subjects visibly suffered from feelings of guilt. Nowadays such experiments would be unthinkable due to strict ethical guidelines.

Minority influence

In addition to majority and obedience to authorities, there is also the possibility that the minority may exert social influence on views, values or behavior. According to social psychologist *Serge Moscovici*, minority influence is the decisive factor when it comes to innovation or social change. The majority, on the other hand, stands for traditionalism and stability. An important prerequisite for the minority's success in exerting social influence is that it be unanimous and consistent in its opinion of deviation from the norm. What is crucial here is that the minority's opinion is persistent and unperturbed by pressure from the majority. This consistent appearance gives the majority the impression of credibility. At the same time, however, it is important that the minority does not behave unruly but tries to convince the majority of its own point of view flexibly. In this way, a truly internalized change of attitude can be achieved among the majority.

Muscovici and colleagues conducted an experiment on the influence of minorities that in principle is reminiscent of Asch's influence on the majority. Four actual test subjects and two supposed test subjects formed a group in the experiment. The group was exclusively presented with blue slides in different brightness levels. If the two supposed subjects convincingly claimed that the slides were green, they could convince a small part of the real test subjects of the same opinion. If they did not behave consistently and only sometimes claimed that the slides were green, no influence on the subjects (majority) could be proven.

5.3 Work in groups

Working in groups is essential in many areas of life. The following section deals with the effects of other people's presence on individual performance, group decision-making and group performance in general.

Effects of the pure presence of other people.

The mere presence of other persons can definitely have an influence on the performance of an individual. This depends to a large extent on the difficulty of the task at hand. If you work on an easy task or a highly overlearned task, the presence of others usually leads to an increase in performance. Social psychology calls this process **social relief**. With difficult or insufficiently learned tasks, on the other hand, the mere presence of others has a negative effect on performance. This is called **social inhibition** in social psychology. One explanation for the phenomenon of social relief or inhibition is that the presence of other persons leads to an increased physical state of excitement of the individual. The increased excitement subsequently leads to the fact that dominant reactions are much more likely to be carried out. Dominant reactions in this context are behaviors that can be routinely performed by frequent repetition. However, if the task is complex, new or insufficiently learned, the dominant reaction often does not lead to success and reduces performance.

Suppose you train in tennis every day. If you then have to play tennis in the presence of a group, this is not a problem. On the contrary, the excitement caused by the presence of others helps you to perform well. However, if you train in tennis daily and now have to play football for the first time in the presence of others, your performance will be reduced.

But why is there increased physical excitement in the presence of others? Three factors play an overriding role:

- **Biological factors**: Biology shows that people have an automatic congenital increase in arousal in the presence of others.

- **Distraction**: The presence of others leads to distraction, which in turn leads to an attention conflict. This attentional conflict also increases physical excitement.

- **Evaluation anxiety**: The fear of being evaluated by other people in relation to one's own performance also automatically leads to an increase in arousal.

Decisions in groups

Decisions are usually made after group discussions. An interesting effect that comes to light in group discussions on decisions is **group polarization**. Group polarization means that following a group discussion, the group members hold a more extreme position than they did before the discussion. Furthermore, there is a tendency to join the majority opinion of the group. The numerical majority has some advantages in the decision-making of a group:

- Majority arguments are more numerous. When many members of a group hold a particular position, the majority usually finds more arguments in numerical terms. The mere number of arguments for a position can lead to individual members taking up that position.

- Majority arguments are discussed more frequently. It seems logical that arguments that the majority represent should also be discussed more frequently, as the group can simply provide more information for these arguments. Conversely, this also leads to minority arguments being systematically given less attention.

- Majority arguments are represented by more independent sources. If more than one person is arguing the same argument, the overall effect is more convincing than if one single individual is repeating the same arguments several times. Nevertheless, this is only true if the persons of the majority are perceived as truly independent.

- Majority arguments are presented more convincingly. It is easier to argue from a majority. As a member of the majority, it is known that most other members of the group take a similar view, which can have a positive effect on the persuasiveness and style of argumentation. Deviators, on the other hand, often appear more insecure in their style of argumentation because they may find their outsider role uncomfortable.

The fact that the majority has such an advantage in decision-making harbors certain risks of making bad decisions. One problem that can arise in the group discussion is **group thinking**. In group thinking, the will to make a consensually shared decision is so important that important counterarguments and facts are simply ignored. Group thinking is encouraged by several conditions. Therefore, factors such as high group cohesion, isolation from alternative sources of information or high stress promote group thinking. A decision based on group thinking is usually of little value because it does not reflect the real viewpoints of the individual members. To avoid group thinking, it is important to have a well-structured discussion in which all relevant information can be heard. It is also helpful if the final vote on a decision is made in secret.

Group performance

In general, group work is expected to improve performance. The increase in performance is measured by the extent to which the group exploits its **group potential**. The group potential describes the performance that all group members would have achieved independently of each other in individual work. The group potential is determined differently depending on the type of task. For **additive tasks** (e.g. shoveling snow) it is the sum of the performance of the individual members. For **subjunctive tasks** (e.g. relay) the group potential is determined by the weakest member. For subjunctive tasks, all group members must perform a minimum performance. **Disjunctive tasks** (e.g. problem solving) are once again different. Here the group potential is determined by the best performance of an individual member. If one now compares the group potential with the actual group performance, one knows whether the group work was a gain or loss for the result.

What dangers lurk in group work that inhibit performance?

A danger can be found in the **coordination of the group**. Poor coordination can lead to an unclear distribution of tasks within a group. No one really knows what to do. Some things are done twice, others not at all. Furthermore, it can happen that members of the group are assigned tasks that do not correspond with their strengths. A final coordination problem can result from poor communication.

A further performance-inhibiting danger, which is observed time and time again in groups, is the loss of motivation. There are various processes that contribute to such a **loss of motivation**.

- **Social free-riding**: If a group member is of the opinion that the group is strong enough to achieve the desired goal without his or her own involvement, this can lead to a strong loss of motivation on the part of the individual. A reduced effort and/or apathy are the result.

- **Social laziness:** If the contribution of the individual in the group work is not clearly recognizable, this can lead to the situation of an individual group member exerting himself less.

- **The idiot effect**: The idiot effect is the reduced effort of the individual for fear of being the only one making an effort at all. In this case, the individual does not want to be the only "idiot" who makes an effort. This feeling of being exploited has an extremely demotivating effect.

This loss of motivation is countered by potential **gains in motivation** through group work:

- **Social compensation:** In well-functioning groups, in which the achievement of goals plays the most important role for the individual group members, it can be observed that high performers often put in more effort than they would in individual work. Their goal is to balance out the performance of the weaker members.

- **Köhler effect**: The so-called Köhler effect works similarly but refers to the weaker group members. These work harder in group work than they would in individual work, since they do not want to be held responsible for poor group performance. The Köhler effect can especially be observed when group membership is very important for the individual.

- **Social competition**: If, within the group, it is clear who is responsible for what performance, a motivating competition between the group members can be created. Each member wants to do better than the others, which can be highly motivating and performance-enhancing.

Another important factor for group performance is good **leadership**. The style of leadership depends on the particular situation. Thus, sometimes a **task-**

oriented leadership style is more effective, whereas another time a **relationship-oriented** leadership style, leading to a feeling of togetherness, is preferable. It is important that the leader assesses the situation correctly and finds a good balance between both leadership styles.

C H A P T E R 6

Intergroup processes

Social psychology speaks of intergroup processes whenever it examines the experience and behavior between groups. Intergroup behavior is characterized by the relative equality of behavioral patterns, attitudes etc. of the individual group members.

6.1 Intergroup perception

The mutual perception between groups essentially occurs via **stereotypes.** Stereotypes are socially shared beliefs about attitudes, character traits, and behavioral patterns etc. that characterize the members of a group. Stereotypes about one's own group are called

autostereotypes and stereotypes about another group are **heterostereotypes.**

The term **prejudice** is used to evaluate the members of a social group. This assessment can be positive or negative in nature and is based on the stereotypical character traits, values and behavioral patterns etc.

Social discrimination is what social psychologists describe as the disadvantage or complete rejection of individuals based on them being a member of a certain group.

The term **stigma** stands in a close relationship to social discrimination. A stigma is a negative attribute through which the bearer of the attribute is subject to social discrimination. This can include external attributes, such as a disfigured face, but also non-visible attributes, such as your sexual orientation. A stigma leads the viewer to believe the carrier has a number of other negative traits, which eventually leads to discrimination, prejudices and disregarding.

What are the functions of stereotypes?

Henri Tajfel, in his analysis on stereotypes, highlights a number of social functions thereof:

- **Positive differentiation:** Positive differentiation of stereotypes has the intended effect of distinguishing the own group from another in a positive way. This is done by using attributes in which the own group is evidently superior to the other group. If, for instance, you want to distinguish yourself positively from foreigners as a German, you could point out their inferior or your superior knowledge of the German language.

- **Causal explanation**: Causal explanations for social events and phenomenon are derived from stereotypes. "Long-term unemployed are basically lazy, otherwise they would not be unemployed for such a long time," would be an example of such an explanation.

- **Social justification**: Stereotypes are used to socially justify the treatment of members of another group. For example, the holding of slaves could be justified by the fact that slaves themselves would not be capable of a better life anyway because they lack the necessary intelligence.

Furthermore, stereotypes are used as a so-called **legitimizing myth**. A legitimizing myth serves to justify the existing differences in power and status between groups.

What are the contents of stereotypes?

Fiske and colleagues have developed an interesting model for the content of stereotypes: The **stereotype content model.** According to the model, the attribution of characteristics depends on two specific characteristics of the intergroup relationship: the intergroup competition (Does the foreign group compete with your own group?) and the status relationship between the two groups (Is the status of the foreign group higher or lower than that of your own group?). These two dimensions result in the following stereotypes:

- **Paternalistic stereotypes**: If the competition is low and the status of the foreign group is low, one speaks of paternalistic stereotypes. Groups exemplifying this would be: pensioners, housewives, disabled people, etc.

- **Despicable stereotypes:** If the competition is high and the status of the foreign group is low, one speaks of despicable stereotypes. Groups exemplifying this are: unemployed, welfare recipients, etc.

- **Admiring stereotypes**: If the competition is low and the status of the foreign group is high, one speaks of admiring stereotypes. Groups exemplifying this are: celebrities, athletes, etc.

- **Envious stereotypes:** If competition is high and the status of the foreign group is also high, one speaks of envious stereotypes. Groups exemplifying this are: Jews, Asian immigrants, etc.

What effects do stereotypes, prejudices and stigmatization have on those affected?

Becoming the target of stereotypes, prejudices or stigmatization can have serious consequences for those affected. Members of a socially disadvantaged group, for example, are much more likely to be victims of both physical and verbal violence. There is evidence that those affected rarely have access to good educational facilities and, despite comparable benefits, can learn less money than those from non-disadvantaged groups. In addition, they receive less medical care and sometimes suffer greatly from the psychological consequences of this unequal treatment. Self-esteem and general psychosocial well-being, for instance, can be severely disrupted. This is particularly true for people who are discriminated against because of their group affiliation but who do not see themselves as part of this group.

Stereotypes, prejudices and stigmatization also affect performance and career choices. Socially devalued groups are afraid of being constantly evaluated on the basis of their group membership. This leads to general nervousness, which can also affect performance in an exam situation. The performance shown in situations like that does not correspond to the actual performance potential. *Eller and Dauhenheimer* conducted an interesting field experiment in this regard. They had girls in sixth grade take a mathematics test while split into two groups. One of the groups received a normal test, while the experimental group received the same one with a preliminary remark. In this preliminary remark, it was pointed out the tasks for the test were specifically selected due to them showing gender-specific differences. These girls, therefore, were confronted with the stereotype that girls usually do worse in mathematics than boys. The pupils in the experimental group indeed showed significantly worse results than the controlled group. The preliminary remarks generated such negative emotions that the students in the experimental group actually performed worse in this test following a sort of self-fulfilling prophecy.

6.2 Causes of intergroup conflicts

Prejudices, stereotypes and stigmatization often lead to group conflicts and exacerbate them.

According to social psychology, what other causes of conflicts between groups still exist?

An easy to understand reason for intergroup conflicts is negative **interdependence**. Negative interdependence means nothing other than that a conflict results from the fact that the goals of one's own group are not compatible with the goals of another. If this is the case negative prejudices between the groups can be aggravated. This often results in hostile or aggressive behavior. The situation appears to negative interdependent groups as: "Your loss is my profit. And your profit is my loss."

Sherif and colleagues conducted the so-called **summer camp studies** on negative interdependence. They created a competition between two neighboring groups of about 12-year-old boys. The competitions were mostly simple games such as tug of war. The winner of the competition then received a reward, while the loser received nothing at all. Pretty quickly an aggressive and hostile atmosphere developed between the previously peaceful groups. Both groups were also constantly engaged in physical and verbal duels outside the competitions. If the conditions were then changed in such a way that cooperation between groups led to a reward for both groups, they interacted in a substantially more peaceful way. Similar findings could also be replicated in other social contexts, such as working groups in companies.

Another cause that can lead to intergroup conflicts is **relative deprivation**. Relative deprivation means that someone has less than they think they deserve. Relative deprivation occurs especially often in social comparison, which can lead to great dissatisfaction among those affected. In intergroup comparison, this phenomenon is called fraternal relative deprivation (comparison between one's own group and a foreign group). It is interesting to note that even individuals who do not feel disadvantaged themselves participate in conflicts when their own group feels disadvantaged. Relative deprivation is a frequent cause of conflicts between groups.

A third cause of intergroup conflicts is a perceived **negative social identity**. If the need for a positive social identity is violated, conflicts may arise between groups. Through social comparison processes people come to the result of a positive or negative social identity. If this result is negative, people try to change it. One way to achieve a change of social identity is social competition. Here, the status-low group challenges the status-higher group with the goal of causing a social change. This challenge can take the form of a simple competition, a collective protest, or even a revolution.

6.3 Reducing prejudices via group contact

How can prejudices and hostilities between groups be reduced?

Gordon Allport, a psychologist, gave the most influential answer to this question to date: Prejudices can be reduced by common, equal contact between majority and minority when pursuing common goals. This so-called **contact hypothesis** was subsequently further developed by other psychologists. *Thomas Pettigrew* concluded and expanded the contact hypothesis to include a number of contact conditions that can lead to a reduction in prejudices between groups:

- **Common overarching goals:** Overarching goals are goals pursued by both groups. The common goals can lead to the groups concerning themselves with the foreign group again and thus experiencing a new point of view of the foreign group through cooperation and solidarity.

- **Cooperation**: It is important that the objectives can only be achieved through cooperation and that competition between the groups is excluded. There is ample evidence of the effectiveness of cooperation reducing prejudice and hostility towards the foreign group.

- **Equal status**: In order to reduce negative assumptions about the foreign group, it is also important that the two groups do not differ in status. If a clear difference in status between the two groups continues to be recognized during contact, there is a danger that stereotypical patterns will continue to be followed.

- **Authorities, norms and laws**: Institutions and authorities can formulate rules and laws that support the interaction between the two groups. Group with a lower status particularly benefit from a legally guaranteed equality of both groups.

- **Potential for friendship**: The formation of intergroup friendships also has the power to break down prejudices and hostilities. Those who offer friendship to members of a foreign group usually have an overall less prejudiced view of the entire foreign group.

If the contact conditions listed above are fulfilled, this can contribute to a change of attitude towards the foreign group. One problem that needs to be overcome is the transfer of positive experiences with individual members of the foreign group to the whole group. Only when the individual succeeds in generalizing the experiences he has made is the reduction of prejudices really successful.

6.4 Prosocial behavior between groups

If you look at what has been said about intergroup processes so far, you might conclude that there are only negative relationships between different groups. While intergroup conflicts are indeed an important social problem, there are also examples of prosocial intergroup behavior. You have most likely seen demonstrations against xenophobia or heard of fundraisers for victims of natural disasters around the world.

What is the difference between helping a foreign group and helping your own group?

As it turns out there are other **motivational processes** behind helping members of a foreign group and helping members of your own. **Empathy** plays an important role in this regard. Research shows that empathy motivates people to help. It is therefore regarded as altruistic motivation. It is, however, proven that empathy is felt much more frequently towards members of one's own group than towards members of a foreign group. This is because it is easier for the individual to feel compassion, sympathy and pity based on the higher similarity to members of their own group. It is easier to put oneself into the same situation with members of one's own group in comparison to foreign group members. Since there is no similarity to foreign group members, people rarely help them for empathic reasons. Here, help is much more systematic and based on **cost-benefit calculations.** Thus, if you expect benefits from helping a member of a foreign group, you are more inclined to help.

Stürmer, Snyder and colleagues were able to confirm this phenomenon in an impressive way in an experiment. In this experiment, it was simulated that the subjects were chatting to another person. The test subjects were male students of German or Muslim descent. The chat partner told the test subjects that he was going through a difficult time. He had just moved to a new town, therefore had no friends and had problems finding an apartment. His current place of residence was only temporary, and he would not be able to live there much longer. The same exact story was presented to all test subjects. Only the name of the chat person varied. For one half of the test persons the chat partner was called Markus, for the other half if was Mohammed. This was to manipulate group membership. During the conversations, the helpfulness and empathy of the test persons was then captured to help the chat partner with the search for accommodation or in any other way. The result was simple: both the German and the Muslim test subjects were much more willing to help a member of their own group than one of the foreign group. As expected, the mediating factor was empathy.

Which functions are fulfilled by helping a foreign group?

The **individual expectation of benefits** is of enormous importance, especially when it comes to long-term help such as voluntary work. The benefit lies in the fact that various individual needs are satisfied by the engagement. The motivations can be of the most different kinds. They can concern the increase of self-esteem, acquiring knowledge, increasing career opportunities or simply distracting from one's own problems. If the individual needs are sufficiently satisfied by the activity as a volunteer, then this has a positive effect on the duration of the engagement.

In addition to the individual benefit, foreign group help also exists if the own group derives a benefit from it. This can, for instance, serve the **maintenance of power and status differences**. Help is not aimed at giving the foreign group autonomy-oriented support through which it could independently get its problem under control in the long term. The support is dependency oriented. This ensures that the power and status differences between the groups do not shift or even manifest themselves. Furthermore, foreign group help can serve to maintain a **positive social identity**. The motivation behind the help is therefore not altruistic but serves, for example, as an opportunity to appear in a good light in front of others.

What opportunities are there to promote solidarity across groups?

Stephen Reicher and colleagues have identified three aspects that can promote solidarity across groups. According to them, political actors have the following possibilities to support prosocial action across groups:

- **Norms and values:** If a group defines itself through (high) humanitarian norms and values and thereby distinguishes itself from other groups, a lack of solidarity towards a foreign group could question its own positive identity. Politicians have the opportunity to bring these norms and values into people's consciousness.

- **Instrumental interests:** Helping a foreign group can be associated with advantages for the group itself. Political actors could emphasize these advantages to enable more solidarity between groups.

- **Redefinition of group boundaries:** Political actors could also try to highlight the similarities between the two groups in order to dissolve and rearrange the groups so that both groups see themselves as one.

Overall, it can be said that intergroup behavior depends on a number of factors. Goals, interests and norms determine whether groups perceive themselves as competition and act with hostility or whether they cooperate, help each other and show solidarity.

Conclusion

Social psychology is a very interesting discipline of psychology. The experience and behavior of humans in social situations are influenced by an immense number of factors. The realizations achieved through social interaction can have a great impact on your daily social experience and behavior. Hopefully, this introduction to social psychology will provide you with an overview of what social psychology concerns itself with.

Lennart Pröss